YOU ARE

fearfully

and

wonderfully

MADE.

Psalm 139:14

About the Author

Jessica Vaughn's passion is to help others become confident and fearless, and know their identity and worth come from Christ. She inspires and encourages thousands by sharing her own personal struggles, victories, and journey through life. Jessica runs a successful online faith and fitness business. Jessica is also the author of two best-selling books, Know Your Worth and A Worthy Wife. She loves being a wife to her husband, Jon, and spends her free time outside whenever she can, playing golf, hiking, reading, and writing. Jessica has a heart after Jesus and credits everything she has done to her Savior.

Facebook: www.facebook.com/jessvaughn22
Website: www.fitcoachjessica.com

Design by Jess Creatives
Edited by Jodi Brandon

The following versions of the Bible were used as scripture sources:
The Message Bible
ESV Bible
NKJ Bible

A Note from the Author:

When God tells us to rise, it's easy for us to tell Him what we lack. He says, "Go." Our response is usually filled with a lot of objections and reasons why we shouldn't.

Friend, I want to remind you (as I sit here and remind myself, too) that our obedience and surrender should be done daily. You won't always see the fruit from your actions. I know that can be frustrating, and can make you feel like you are not good enough or doing a good job. Just know that when you act out of surrender and obedience, you store up treasures in heaven so that when you see Jesus face-to-face He can say, "Well done, my good and faithful servant."

Have faith that trusts Him more than you could ever trust yourself. Don't get so distracted by this world that you lose your identity in everything but Him. Your life is an adventure—an adventure meant to be taken with Him.

You will never be in a better place than in His arms, on His lap, and giving your life over to Him.

You are loved. You are worthy. You are enough.

You are worthy,
Jessica

How to Use This Journal

This journal is designed so that you can write whatever you want, whenever you want. There is no start date or end date. There is no need to feel like you are behind in writing or that you need to be consistent every day. Although I highly recommend you coming back to your journal on a regular basis, don't feel the pressure to write every day (especially if you are just getting used to journaling).

I know how often thoughts of inadequacy can come up. Sometimes it's moment-to-moment and even more intense and more often when you start to do work for the Kingdom. Come back to this journal as often as you can to write down the lies, then cross them out and replace them with the truth. His truth. Repeat the truth out loud if you have to.

Go to God and get intimate with Him in this journal. Our worth will never come from anything in this world. Write what you feel. Be honest about it.

I encourage you to always self-reflect when writing. Ask the Lord to show you what's going on in your heart above all else. Whenever you get out on paper what you need to get out, always end with hope and encouragement to yourself.

I want you to know there are no rules when it comes to writing. Just write. Write whatever comes to your mind and let it flow out onto the paper.

7 Tips for Journaling

Find a space where you feel comfortable to write. A space where you can focus and concentrate. Don't overthink this.

Ask yourself questions. If you are ever unsure of what to write, ask yourself questions. It helps you to reflect on the day or week you have had. For example: What happened today? How did it make you feel?

Time yourself. It's easy to get lost in writing sometimes. Setting a timer can help you stay focused and productive, especially if you're new to journaling.

Date your entry. Don't forget to put a date down on the paper whenever you begin to write. There is nothing better than going back through your journals to see where you were on specific days and how far you have come.

Write honestly. Write as if no one would ever see what you have written. Don't lie to yourself. That doesn't help you. Journaling can be very therapeutic. A lot of self-discovery can happen when you are open and honest with what's going on inside.

Write quickly. Don't give yourself time to think about it. Just let the words flow and see what kind of writing follows.

Write naturally. Don't think about it. Don't try to have form or structure. Let your thoughts come to paper. Don't worry if they are all out of order and all over the place. This isn't an English paper.

Jesus traveled through Samaria and found a woman, during the hottest part of the day, at a well. She was there because she knew that no one else would be there.

She hesitated. She questioned. She tried to dodge the situation. She was confronted by a man who didn't judge her. A man who spoke to her, even though normally if a man spoke to a woman in this time she would have considered herself shamed.

Although Jesus was tired from His journey, He never hesitated to show the kind of love she deserved and the kind of water that will never make her thirst again.

He loves you just the same.

He'll never get tired of stopping to show you and express His love for you.

God's love isn't performance-based. Once we realize and understand this, it takes us to a new level with Him.

Be real and get quiet with God. Don't try to hide what He already knows. It's not about what we do, it's about who He is!

No checklist will bring peace, contentment, forgiveness, and healing like a relationship with God will.

Let's make sure we are intentional about our heart being close to God instead of trying to hold a checklist up against Him for others to see.

Be intentional about the time you spend with Him.

It's easy to see the outside appearance of someone. What really matters is what's going on inside.

You can see abs, how people appear on social media, and all the workout pictures, but you miss their own internal battle and the struggles they face every day that no one knows about.

Don't sacrifice joy, peace, happiness, and love for yourself over a perfect body. It's not worth it!

Focus on your heart toward your workouts above all else. Focus on your eternal relationship with your heavenly Papa.

Don't fixate on a destination, and realize this is the rest of your life. Energy and health over abs and exhaustion!

We find our true
identities when we
spend time in His
word and in His
presence.

"For nothing is hidden that will not be made manifest, nor is anything secret that will not be known and come to light."

– Luke 8:17

I know you may feel hidden, as if no one sees you, even God.

You work hard, you do amazing things, you give it your all, but still it feels like nothing you do is good enough!

When He says nothing is hidden, that means nothing. So, if you are feeling likes no one sees or notices, don't give up. God may have you hidden for a season and a reason.

Don't waste all your energy trying to get noticed. Understand you are here because He wants you to be!

"He is not afraid of bad news; his heart is firm, trusting in the Lord. His heart is steady; he will not be afraid until he looks in triumph on his adversaries."
– Psalm 112:7–9

The world is full of bad news and things happening, but how great is it to know that there's no need to be afraid of it? I pray today that your heart is firm and trusting in the Lord.

Do you have or wear things that remind you to take your focus and eyes back to God?

If you are constantly focused on the number on the scale, stressed about everything you can and can't eat, you are probably missing the big picture!

Step one: Hide the scale.
Step two: Open your Bible.
Step three: Begin to discover your true worth.

"When you look at these tassels you'll remember and keep all the commandments of God, and not get distracted by everything you feel or see that seduces you into infidelities. The tassels will signal remembrance and observance of all my commandments, to live a holy life to God. I am your God who rescued you from the land of Egypt to be your personal God. Yes, I am God, your God."

– Numbers 15:37–41)

Daniel 2:20-22 says,

"*He knows all, does all: He changes the seasons and guides history, He provides both intelligence and discernment, He opens the depths, tells secrets, sees in the dark—light spills out of Him!*"

(This is where Daniel is asking God about the dream King Nebuchadnezzar had.)

You don't need to be afraid to ask for what you need. You don't need to fear for what the future has in store, either. It's all prepared and planned. You don't have to ask Him to be there with you, because Deuteronomy 31:6 tells us, "He will never leave us or forsake us."

Know that the moments you spend with Him define who you become.

So many of us have passion and desires put on our hearts. Yet, many forget that action is required with our faith. (See James 2:17.)

God isn't going to give you the whole picture. He doesn't match His purpose with a bank account status or current circumstance.

Let's not shrink our God to our thinking. Let's raise our thinking to how big our God is.

"Only let each person lead the life that the Lord has assigned to Him and to which God has called him."
– 1 Corinthians 7:17

You are neither equipped nor assigned to lead anyone's life but yours. God has entrusted us with people in our lives, but wishing, hoping, comparing, or resenting someone else for the life God has blessed them with only hinders you from your assignment.

"Come to me, all you who are weary and burdened, and I will give you rest. Take my yoke upon you and learn from me, for I am gentle and humble in heart, and you will find rest for your souls. For my yoke is easy and my burden is light."

– Matthew 11:28–30

Today be reminded of rest. Rest doesn't have to be torture, and it doesn't mean you are not productive.

Let's be reminded that we can't rely on our own strength to get us by. Free yourself from the bondage that says you have to work all the time to have worth.

The more time we spend with Him, the more we become like Him.

"It's not about the path; it's about the person. All of us follow the same person but not all of us follow the same path."

—Judah Smith

Our purpose is so much more important than the pace at which we accomplish something.

Everyone's racing, trying to be the best and at the top, so that sometimes the journey becomes frustrating, unfulfilling, and more about our own glory than giving glory. You can see a great example of purpose over pace in the story of David. He was anointed king but served Saul humbly. (See 1 Samuel 16:21) He was anointed king, but it was not yet his appointed time.

The pace at which you go or how fast you get where He is calling you to go is irrelevant because when the focus is on Him you'll be where you need to be at just the right time.

"We have received grace and apostleship to bring obedience of faith for the sake of His name among nations."

- Romans 1:4–5

Take note of Paul's love, enthusiasm, and straight-forwardness about preaching the gospel with no shame when you are reading in Romans.

I pray for you to be more like Paul. Your story can lead others to Him. No matter the story, it can shine for His glory.

What story can you share with others about His grace and love on your life?

Jesus is the one we
follow. All eyes on Him.

Whatever you are holding on to, let it go from your arms to our Papa's arms. Every time you try to take it back, keep giving it back to Him—over and over again.

_____

_____

_____

_____

_____

_____

_____

_____

_____

_____

_____

_____

_____

_____

_____

_____

_____

_____

_____

_____

_____

_____

_____

"God has given each of you a gift from his great variety of spiritual gifts. Use them well to serve one another."
– 1 Peter 4:10

Feeling unqualified? Feeling like you have no gifts or purpose? 1 Peter 4:10 crushed that thinking: "God has given each of you," not one person left behind or forgotten.

He qualifies us. He has given you something special, and you may just be too close to see it.

Don't try to have it all figured out. Just take the steps of faith and acts of obedience every day, no matter how small, with Him.

"There's a time for everything."
– Ecclesiastes 3:2–8

I know you may be praying and trying to rush through this season, but you are where you are with great purpose and a divine plan.

You and I cannot event begin to comprehend the plans that God has for us. It doesn't mean it will be without pain, disappointment, or heartbreak. It does mean that He never forgets the promises He makes.

Live a life full of risks
rather than a life full of
doubt.

Do you really feel blessed, or have you let yourself feel less than because you have spent more time scrolling and comparing than actually living the life God has given you?

Your life is significant. He calls us all by name. (See Isaiah 43:1.) He doesn't call us by groups, color, race, or ethnicity. He calls us each individually.

"What's so beautiful about our call is that God knows full well whom He's getting when He calls."
—Susie Larson

It's funny how we think that, because of the things we have done or that have been done to us, God can't use us to do amazing things in this world.

Where He guides, He provides.

It's time to start falling in love with your own story instead of wishing for some else's. There's so much glory that can be given to God right now, being exactly who you are.

No one has your story and that makes you extraordinary!

Peter got out of the boat and began to walk toward Jesus on the water. Jesus is the way but in that moment Peter experienced two ways: his eyes focused on the storm raging, which filled him with fear, causing him to sink, and keeping his eyes on Jesus, which allowed him to walk on water.

There are always two ways for us, too: Jesus or the storm.

Out of our storms we can see our character changed and God's blessing more than ever.

Our lives can be messy, confusing, and frustrating, but Jesus and His love say, "Stay focused on me and I'll take care of the storm."

Where's your focus today?

Raise your eyes to Heaven because He's the same God yesterday, today, and tomorrow.

"God created us to move forward. Our bodies are designed to move forward and not backwards. Let's drop this whole two steps forward and one step back because God didn't design us to move backwards."
—Kris Vallotton

Despite the circumstance, let's have the courage to move forward. Constantly move forward even when you think everything is being stripped down in your life. Keep moving forward!

Many of us live a poverty life, and I'm not referring to money.

Lack of courage. Lack of faith. Lack of love. Lack of boldness. Lack of strength.

We live more in lack than we do in abundance.

The poverty life leaves us with doubt. And doubt attracts attack. The enemy wants to be your ally. He wants you to live this poverty life so you can't fully embrace the life God has for you. He'll have you convinced your nothing and not worth anything. Then, your actions and decisions proceed with that lie.

Don't waste another second thinking you have to live this poverty life anymore, because you don't!

Your life is going to be consumed with so many unsure moments—moments where you aren't sure where to go or what to do next. The thing you do know is that God runs the show.

Our days will be full of a lot of "yesterdays" before we know it, and we will have very few tomorrows.

If you have been waiting to go after that goal or dream, then do it. If you want to get healthier, then make the decision tonight and not tomorrow. If you want to be happy, then create your happy if your life seems anything but that.

It's not impossible. Yes, it may be tough. But you're tough! You have God on your side.

It's your choice to live. Live today. Live well.

"A peaceful heart leads to a healthy body; jealousy is like cancer in the bones."

– Proverbs 14:30

When was the last time you thanked God for everything He has blessed you with? Blessing doesn't just mean money or things. Blessings could even mean some of the not-so-joyful-feeling seasons.

We see in Proverbs that jealousy is like cancer in the bones. It begins to slowly kill us and our dreams because we think what others have is better than what we have. God doesn't have favorites. He doesn't just have a plan for you; He has a purpose for you.

Let's pray for your journey today with Him. Let's have that peaceful heart knowing He designed that journey just for you.

"If you want to be miserable, try to make God fit into your world. If you want joy, find your place in His world."
— Michelle Myers

It's easy to find the need to rush into a new adventure after just completing one. The feelings that you aren't doing enough begin to rise, and you have to remind yourself of the truth.

In a world in which we are being told it's never enough or we are never enough, let's make sure our focus goes back to the One who is enough and all that we need. You are enough!

Hebrews 13:2 says,

"Do not forget to entertain strangers, for by doing so some have unwittingly entertained angels."

You have the opportunity to entertain angels as you live moment-to-moment. Do you really know the people with whom you come in contact?

We see angels appear to Abraham in Genesis. They appear to Mary in Luke. (And many other times throughout the Bible.) There is no reason not to believe that today you can entertain angels. Especially since "He is the same God as yesterday and today!" (Hebrew13:8)

So, the next time you think no one sees, cares, or notices, just remember that the next person you encounter could in fact be an angel!

Let's have hearts that look for it and expect it!

Rest your fast-paced, ex-
hausted, tired self. Let's
not confuse it with doing
nothing. Let's makes sure
our rest is in Him.

_____
_____
_____
_____
_____
_____
_____
_____
_____
_____

_____

_____ *"I have called you by*
_____ *your name; you are mine."*
_____ – Isaiah 43:1
_____
_____ *"Because you are*
_____ *precious in my sight and*
_____ *honored, and because I*
_____ *love you."*
_____ – Isaiah 43:4
_____
_____ When you have mini-moments
_____ of identity crisis (meaning when
_____ you are allowing yourself to be
_____ swayed by things/people other
_____ than Jesus), reign yourself back
_____ in by remembering how deep
_____ His love is and how faithful He is
_____ when we honor Him.
_____
_____ It's easy to get off track but simple
_____ to get back on.

There will be seasons during which it will seem like nothing is happening—that everything you are doing isn't making an impact or doesn't matter.

Don't determine your success based on worldly applause. Quiet seasons don't mean it's time to quit.

He blesses our motives and heart, regardless of any outcome!

I don't know what your worry or concern is today. I don't know the struggle you face or what is weighing you down.

But I do want to share this question with you and pray it will encourage you: Will this matter in eternity? If you have enough time to worry, you have enough time to pray.

You have a choice about what lens you choose to view your life from. We can't see His purpose without His perspective.

_____

_____

_____

_____

_____

_____

_____

_____

_____

_____

_____

_____

_____

_____

_____

_____

_____

_____

_____

_____

_____

_____

_____

"No, in all these things we are more than conquerors through him who loved us. For I am sure that neither death nor life, nor angels nor rulers, nor things present nor things to come, nor powers, nor height nor depth, nor anything else in all creation, will be able to separate us from the love of God in Christ Jesus our Lord.."

– Romans 8:37–39

Nothing separates us from His love regardless of your relationship status. It's not more love for the singles or more blessing for the married. You are loved. Period.

You are stronger than what your past is trying to remind you of!

You have a history. It's okay; we all do. But let's break from the shame and guilt that hold us back from using it for His glory and our purpose!

Peter was in prison for preaching the Word. The very same night an angel appeared and woke Peter, and the chains fell off his hands. (See Acts 12:7.)

You may be putting yourself in prison right now—shackled by your past and covered in shame. You have created your own prison that you have locked yourself in.

Peter had soldiers and sentries guarding that prison, and the chains still broke and he was freed.

Nothing you have done, nor anything done to you, is too much or too bad for our God.

Praying that you be delivered and freed from the prison you have put yourself in. He is our chain breaker!

He created you and me not because He had to, but because He wanted to.

"Oh taste and see that the Lord is good; Blessed is the man who trusts in Him."

– Psalm 34:8

Hold on to His promises today. Know that everything God created was with purpose and intention.

Sometimes you just have to remember how far you have come! Take a moment to give God glory for all that you have been through. You have been refined by the fire!

_____

_____

_____

_____

_____

_____

_____

_____

_____

_____

_____

_____

_____

_____

_____

_____

_____

_____

To-do lists, unnecessary stress and worry, overwhelmed schedule—feel any of these? Although they don't just disappear, we are given the strength to overcome them and put them back in their place.

You are the daughter/son of the King because He is the kings of kings. (See Revelation 19:16.) Your life isn't meant to be run by yes's to just please others.

Don't miss the things that matter because you were focused on the things that didn't matter!

You are so blessed. He doesn't make any mistakes!

You don't go through what you go through for punishment. Some outcomes you experience may be from your own free will choices, but when you go through something so hard, you realize it's not for punishment but to make you stronger, more confident, and bolder in faith.

I pray you begin to change the way you view your circumstance and remember that you are never alone. The enemy only wants you to feel alone.

If you stay in the victim role forever, you'll never be able to taste the freedom that He gives.

We often compare and compete because we have the mindset that there isn't enough or God has favorites. God doesn't have favorites. He is waiting to lift you up. Often, we don't allow ourselves to step into the blessings of God!

Let's spend less time comparing and more time lifting others up!

God is a big God and His
blessings continue to
overflow every day!

Obedience usually comes with a price. Obedience often looks different because it goes against the rules and regulations the world has tried to set for us. Obedience often makes us extremely uncomfortable, sometimes has us question our capability, and doesn't always come with big, pretty bows.

Say yes to more things that bring you joy and where you feel the tug to go.

Say yes to God.

"It's not my work, it's God's work.
I'm just the pencil in His hand."
—Mother Theresa

Rise up!

When will you stop feeling sorry for yourself? All those inadequate thoughts, all that negative self-talk, all the buts you add into your goals and dreams—all are you feeling sorry for yourself.

If you think about it, we think about ourselves way more than we do anyone else. We think about ourselves more than we think about Jesus and His perspective on things or us. (Ouch!)

Your situations don't define you! Don't let them hold you down anymore.

"Your very lives are a letter that anyone can read by just looking at you. Christ himself wrote it — not with ink, but with God's living Spirit; not chiseled into stone, but carved into human lives — and we publish it."

– 2 Corinthians 3:3

Every day is a new chapter to your life. It doesn't have to be a "different day, same story" kind of day today.

What's powerful is the spirit within us, but we have been so focused on ourselves and what we don't want (or do want) that we can't see what He is calling us to do. Often where He calls us is painful, is uncomfortable, and stretches us.

Even though some days you may feel like a mess and need to get it together, your life can still be a testimony for others.

Praying for you to get out of a spirit of poverty (poor spirit) and into a spirit of wealth. Things, money, ranks, and titles won't make you wealthy in spirit.

Wealthy is an inside job, and your employer is God.

Too many times I have seen people back down, quit, and give up because they are "not lucky like so and so" or they don't want to put any skin in the game.

It's time to dream past your circumstance!

He hasn't left you. He's not punishing you, either.

James 4:10 is a great reminder to read today:

"Humble yourselves in the sight of the Lord, and He will lift you up."

Let God do the talking today, and you listen.

Even when the disciples felt rejected and wanted to give up, the Lord was always there with a reminder to say, "I got you. I love you. I'll protect you. This is your purpose here."

Write to God today and pray about His will for your life as a foot soldier!

What determines your success?

What makes you feel successful?

Three foundational success principles that all of us should have come from Psalm 37:

1. Trust in the Lord and do good.

2. Commit your way to the Lord.

3. Rest in the Lord and wait patiently for Him.

Lord, remove anything that isn't a part of your will for my life. Even if it appears like I am losing, remind me that I am gaining.

"Now the Lord is the Spirit, and where the Spirit of the Lord is, there is freedom."

– 2 Corinthians 3:17

Freedom from:

Calories
Idols
Numbers
Ranks
Titles
Food
And the list goes on.

What is the Lord working on your heart about when it comes to freedom? He's the key to unlocking the places that we try to control and keep for ourselves. I pray you let Him unlock and unpack whatever you are trying to keep away.

Is your faith based on your circumstance?

Is your faith there in the hard times as much as it is the great times?

How do we make our faith not conditional? By laying it all down at His feet. Yes, everything:

Your business.
Your workouts.
Your relationships.

Are you worrying more than you are praying? Are you trying to control the situation or are you lifting it up to God over and over again?

We pray once, we feel like nothing happened, then we give up and think God doesn't care.

Today, write down that worry you have. Then, every time it pops up, give it back to God. Declare it!

It's easy to follow people on social media, and it's easy to fall in love with their message, and it's easy for them to feel like your savior because they have had so much influence over your life.

Remember that they are only a vessel that God is using in this world. Our Savior is the one we all need more than anyone or anything. He is what sustains us and the One who doesn't fail us.

He uses others to show us possibility, not to make us feel inferior or not good enough!

How often do the words "God, I want more of you" come out of your mouth?

It can be challenging because, when you ask for more of Him, you'll discover more of about yourself than you are ready to confront. It can be too uncomfortable.

When you ask for more, you are asking Him to take you to places you have never been before.

You don't grow in what you already know.

Pray for more and be ready for the uncomfortable, knowing it's for our growth and His glory.

Being married doesn't mean your insecurities, selfishness, doubts, fears, or loneliness goes away. If you are single, don't wait for married life to start living your life. If you are married, how can you pray for your husband? More importantly, ask God what areas in your marriage you can improve on. (That is the tough stuff.)

I want you to experience the freedom and the joy you can have when you surrender to the One that created us. Surrender and quit white-knuckling your way through life, and quit trying to control everything and be everything to everybody.

Romans 1:17 instructs us to move faith-to-faith.

It's easy to go faith-to-faith when you are in an awesome season of life. Right? But it's hard to move faith-to-faith when you feel like you hear God wrong or are going through a growing season.

It's more like faith-to-doubt, faith-to-wanting to give up, and then back to faith-to-faith.

Are you moving faith-to-faith like His word encourages us to do regardless of what's going on in your life?

Know that you are authentic. Nobody can tell you how to tell your story. Nobody can tell you how to feel about your story. Nobody can tell you anything about your story except God.

When it comes to loving your body, first think about the non-scale victories. It might be choosing to work out instead of watching Netflix. It could be going out and playing with your kids instead of working a little bit longer. It could be leaving work earlier to go to the gym. You could wake up earlier and go to the gym. Or it could even be spending time with God and learning how to love yourself emotionally. Those are all non-scale victories.

What non-scale victories have you accomplished today?

The scale doesn't determine who you are and who God created you to be. It doesn't determine your gifts, your talents, your kindness, your generosity, or your servanthood. Those are things the scale doesn't weigh. Focus on the non-scale victories today!

_____

_____

_____ What you speak over yourself has power.

_____ The words that you say, become the actions you display.

I'm challenging you today, no matter where you are and no matter what's going on, to pray and ask God to change your perspective of the situation.

Know that your worth comes from Christ. The Lord is your strong foundation. If at times you find yourself caught up in numbers and ranks and people's opinions again, refocus and remember the Lord is your provider. He takes care of you and you are loved.

Proverbs 18:21 says,
"Death and life are in the power of the tongue, and those who love it will eat its fruit."

You will produce what you say!

A match can start a forest fire and a rudder controls a ship. (You see this example in James 3:4.)

Your tongue is so small yet guides the course of action for your life.

The things you say to your spouse matter. The things you say to yourself matter. The things you say to your friends matter. It all matters!

Think about what you are thinking about.

What's amazing is that our mind is usually the culprit behind our fitness or health. Long-term results involve trudging through the deep waters of our own self-love.

It starts there and then our bodies respond. (Of course, every situation is unique.)

It's not that you have to work out, it's that you get to work out.

If your goals this year involve losing weight and getting healthy, remember that it starts with you first: the way you view food, view your workout, and view your body!

You are so much more than a number or a six-pack.

My friend, the work out is the joy not the dread.

"Take every thought into captivity to the obedience of Christ."

– 2 Corinthians 10:6

Half of the time you may not even realize what you are thinking about. It's clear we need to take every thought captive. In other words, is this thought based on truth or a lie? Is it creating fruit in your life? Or, is it hindering you, bringing you down, and making you feel less than?

This is an action step!

There is an enemy that doesn't want to see you succeed. But there is a God who is ready to bless you with cities and nations.

How can you love, if you don't know what love is? Have you ever asked yourself that question?

Everyone has been shown love in a different way and through different experiences. Some have experienced love through beatings, rape, and abuse. Others have been shown love by kind words, hugged like they were cared for, and told they could be anything in this world.

Both sides can view their experience as it being love, because that's what they know and have been shown. You don't know (when you are in it) that being lied to and being told off aren't love.

It's not until you know another side—another perspective: our Savior's love—that we really encounter a love that feels like love. A love that rocks our world to its core and challenges everything we have ever known. A love that is patient, is kind, doesn't boast, doesn't envy, isn't rude, bears all things, believes all things, and hopes all things. (See 1 Corinthians 13:4–7.)

You are loved and you can love. I challenge you to ask God to show you where your love stems from. Is it His love or the love you have been shown?

Forgive yourself. You are not perfect nor will you ever be. It doesn't matter what you did. What matters is where you are going.

Reach for the Word
instead of the world.

The day that you received
Jesus into your heart was the
first day of your ministry.

Instead of asking what is my purpose. Start asking yourself, "Why do I feel like I don't have a purpose?"

If you don't have God's perspective you will never see His purpose.

Made in the USA
San Bernardino, CA
26 January 2018